APERTURE
Volume 18, Number 3 & 4 (a combined issue)
Minor White   Editor
Michael E. Hoffman   Managing Editor/Publisher
Jonathan Green   Associate Editor
Stevan A. Baron   Production
Véronique Lipsey   Designer

Aperture, Inc., publishes *Aperture*
intermittently at Millerton, New York 12546.
Officers include President, Minor White;
Vice-President/Treasurer, Michael E. Hoffman;
and Secretary, Arthur M. Bullowa.
Directors include the Officers,
Shirley C. Burden and Robert A. Hauslohner.
The entire contents are copyright © 1974
by Aperture, Inc. Regular subscriptions are
$17.50 for four issues in the United States
and $18.50 in U.S. currency in Canada and
foreign countries. Retaining subscriptions are $50.00.
Sustaining subscriptions are $100.00 or more.
Of these amounts $17.50 covers the cost of
four issues: the remainder is in the nature of
a gift to help support an ideal in photography—
such gifts are tax deductible. The names of
retaining and sustaining subscribers are
published for the duration of their
special subscriptions.

Ralph Eugene Meatyard

Ralph Eugene Meatyard

Edited with text by James Baker Hall

Reminiscence by Guy Davenport

an Aperture Monograph

I wish to express my thanks to Michael Hoffman and Minor White for their help in the preparation of this book; and to Madelyn and Christopher Meatyard, and Bob May. And most especially to Shawn Watson, whose understanding of Gene Meatyard's work, and much else besides, has been an inspiration to me; the retrospective show of his photographs that she hung at Matrix in Hartford served as a model for the selection and sequencing of the images in this book.
J.B.H.

James Baker Hall, a photographer and a writer, was a friend of Gene Meatyard's. This monograph was begun in 1970, with Meatyard's approval, and finished after his death, with his wife Madelyn's assistance and blessing. Hall has been experimenting for some time now with more or less uncommon ways to bring words and pictures together; his text here, a series of free-floating prose poems based on his observations of Meatyard as a man and as an artist and on certain of his own childhood experiences, attempts to create a context in which the photographer's vision will be more readily accessible. Hall has taught photography at M.I.T. and at the University of Connecticut; his pictures have been published and exhibited widely. He is the author of a novel, *Yates Paul, His Grand Flights, His Tootings,* and numerous stories, poems, articles, and reviews which have appeared in such magazines as *Popular Photography, Esquire, The Saturday Evening Post, The New York Quarterly, Field,* and *Place.* Currently he is teaching creative writing at the University of Kentucky.

Guy Davenport, also a friend of Meatyard's, provides a reminiscence. Poet, story writer, critic, scholar, translator, he is the author of *The Intelligence of Louis Agassiz, Carmina Archilochi, Sappho,* and a book of poems, *Flowers and Leaves*; a volume of his short stories entitled *Tatlin!* will be published soon by Scribner's. His articles and reviews have appeared in such periodicals as *The Hudson Review, The New York Times Book Review, Life,* and *Poetry.* He is a Professor of English at the University of Kentucky.

The design is by Véronique Lipsey.
The photographs were sequenced by James Baker Hall.

The Family Album of Lucybelle Crater with photographs by Ralph Eugene Meatyard and text by Jonathan Williams and others will be published in 1974 by The Jargon Society. It is available from the distributor, The Book Organization, Elm Street, Millerton, New York 12546.

Aperture, Inc., publishes a Quarterly of Photography, portfolios, and books to communicate with serious photographers and creative people everywhere. A catalog of publications is available upon request.

Published in the United States by Aperture, Inc., Elm Street, Millerton, New York 12546 and simultaneously in Europe by McGraw-Hill Book Company GmbH, Dusseldorf, Germany, and in Canada by Gage Trade Publishing, Agincourt, Ontario.

Library of Congress Catalog Card Number 74-76879
ISBN Numbers: Clothbound 912334-62-2
                            Paperbound 912334-61-4
Manufactured in the United States of America.
Printed by Rapoport Printing Corp., and bound by Sendor Bindery.

Emblems & Rites

Ralph Eugene Meatyard is Eyeglasses of Kentucky in the Imperial Plaza Shopping Center in Lexington, 1969.

He's at his workbench in the back room of his new shop on Saturday morning with a cup of tea and the radio. He is waiting, as patiently as a bird watcher, for business. He had a good job at Tinder-Krauss-Tinder, but he always wanted a shop of his own. A small one-way peek window lets him watch the shop and the shopping center parking lot and the hospital across the street. There are U.S.G.S. maps of the Red River Gorge on the wall above the workbench. Lexington is polluting Elkorn Creek all the way to Georgetown. The prosecuting attorney of Fayette County would like to see all the liberal professors at the University fired. The receptionist sits at the desk near the front door and files her nails. On the table in the waiting area are magazines: U.S. News and World Report, Sports Illustrated, The Hudson Review, Kayak, *and the issue of* Monk's Pond *containing his thirteen-year-old son's first published poem. There's an exhibition of his photographs on the walls of the shop. Two carloads of students and professors from Ohio are coming in the afternoon when the shop is closed to see the show and to meet him. The radio plays, softly,* NBC News on the Hour. *His "Murcan Law," one of the several junk sculptures and constructs he keeps there in the workroom, is a road sign, streaked with white bird droppings, that says* WALK ON THIS SIDE, *a toy red bird perched on top, its head painted blue; and his "Murcan Religion" is a dismembered doll crucified on a piece of driftwood. His hobby is collecting strange names from newspapers and phone books and magazines and other sources he deems reliable: Lummy Jean Licklighter, T. Bois Dangling, Jr., Margaret A. Ditto Ditto, Pharoh Feeback and Connie Fongdong, Everette Derryberry and Decimus Ultimus, five brothers named Ecton, Chansman, Shanch, Sell, and James — each verified by an address and kept neatly listed in a small brown loose-leaf notebook. He won't let his thirteen-year-old son, Christopher, make five dollars washing the plate-glass windows of Eyeglasses of Kentucky on Saturday morning again until he cuts his hair. He would go out and talk to the receptionist except he wants to appear busy. In front of him on the workbench the decapitated head of a pink doll is set on a pedestal of boxes containing his pictures of the Red River Gorge. Waiting for business he entertains himself by tapping the doll's head lightly with a tack hammer and watching her expression change.*

There is a story about an anonymous naval photographer whose job during World War II was to film the take-offs and the landings of carrier-based planes. Although it was a routine assignment, he believed that it was charged with moral urgency, and he devoted himself to it accordingly. One day a bomb detached itself from a returning plane just as it touched down and bounced across the flight deck toward him. Everyone except the photographer ran for his life. The footage, which survived, showed how he stood his ground, absorbed in his job, how he kept the bomb perfectly framed as it bounced wildly across the deck toward him.

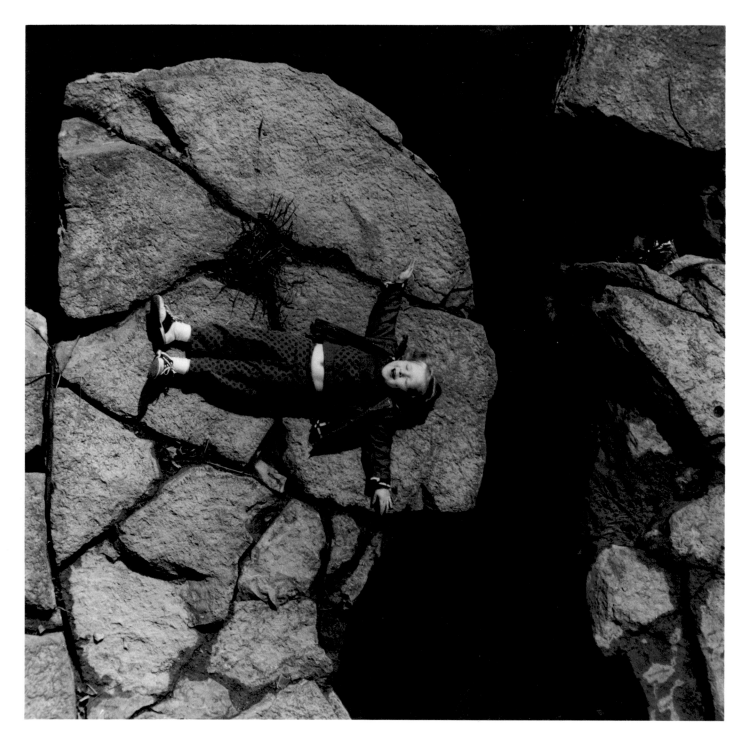

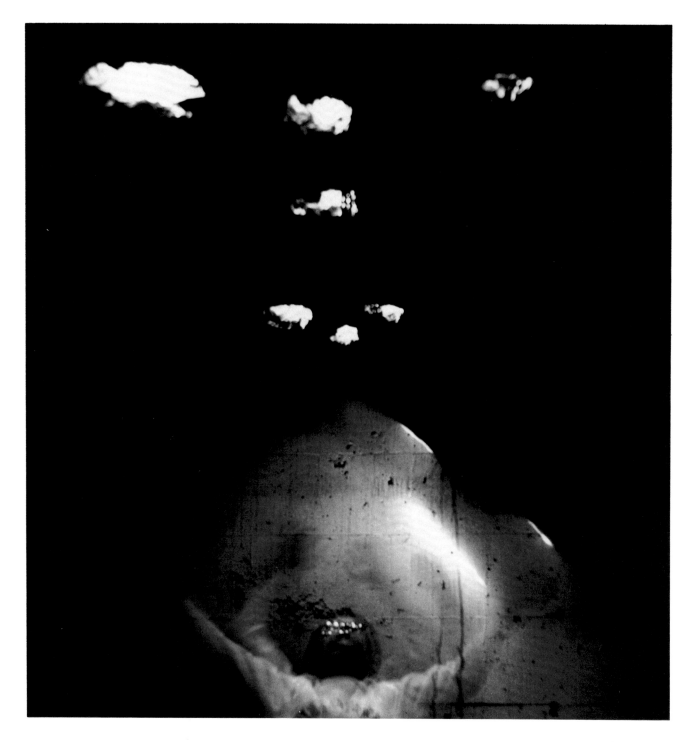

What it's like to be an artist in Kentucky.

        If the women on the porch swing are hostile when they see your camera, you can imagine what's going on inside. It's Lucybelle Crater, and her friend, Lucybelle Crater. That's what it's like to be an artist in Kentucky.

        In the right setting, anything can happen. Picture what a pair like that would do! Picture Lucybelle Crater and her friend, Lucybelle Crater! That's what it's like to be an artist in Kentucky. You're Lucybelle Crater, and her friend, Lucybelle Crater.

Gene's vending machine:
you-all come in, have a chair—there's one hanging on the wall there.

        An old cane bottom, the broken legs still hanging on,
decorated by a dismembered doll; the bright-eyed head impaled on one upright,
the pink body on the other; her pink legs high booties for the chair legs; her pink
arms calling out from the cane bottom for help.
        You'd be wise to decline, observing that the chair is
occupied, by a furious child shaking a tall weed furiously on a dark hillside above
a country church in the south.

Hold it now.

        According to the father's instructions, the son is
holding a knife-shaped shard of mirror against his face so that it backs light, just
so. The father, preoccupied with his vision, ignores the son's tiring arms.
        They're trying, they're both trying, but they end up
screaming at one another.
        It's a cold Sunday afternoon in a deserted house in a
cornfield in Kentucky: broken windows, graffiti, women in the shadows. There are
fathers and sons elsewhere, in filling stations and on fishing trips, pretending not
to hear.

I remember the cold wood floor under my feet when I got up at night and went into my grandparents' bedroom to drink out of the silver pitcher that sat in the window sill; I remember the sound of the crickets, and the moonlight on the pasture, and the sound of my grandparents sleeping there in the room behind me; I remember writing my name in the cold sweat on the pitcher and then erasing it hurriedly as soon as the letters started to leak.

And I remember standing at the same window just before sunup waiting for Ed Gibbs, the colored handyman, to come to work; I remember the feel of Ed Gibbs' callused hands, the stains on his teeth, the tools and the rags in the rumble seat of his old car where he would let me play sometimes as a treat; I remember standing on the seat beside him with my arm around his neck when he drove my grandmother to town, and I remember the smell of the sweatband on his chauffeur's hat, which my grandmother didn't like me to put on; and I remember stealing a dollar from my grandmother's purse and trying to give it to Ed under the grape arbor around the cistern in the backyard.

I remember taking a bath with my mother; I remember sitting in the tub with my legs stuck out straight between hers; and I remember touching once with my toes, touching briefly with my toes, the great bush of floating black hair between her legs. I remember being told that I had to play very quietly, for my mother was sick; I remember hiding behind a door one night when she was well enough to come down to supper, and I remember jumping out and scaring her; and I remember that she tried to stay and eat with us but had to leave and go back to her room.

And I remember begging my father, whenever he was home, to shoot bats at dusk in the front yard, and I remember the excitement when he got out the shotgun; and I remember the smell of the empty green and red shells that he let me keep afterwards.

I want to get this exactly right. Ed Gibbs is up in the tree with a saw. I'm playing on the ladder underneath him. When the gun goes off, he knows immediately what has happened, and he says "Oh my God! Miss Lurline! Miss Lurline!" and drops to the ground and runs for the house. I'm afraid to follow him, afraid to be left alone.

So I am standing in the doorway to my mother's room: she is lying on the far twin bed under the window, the front of her nightgown is matted with blood; she is staring straight up at the ceiling; she is breathing heavily. The organdy curtains billow out softly over the foot of the bed. My grandmother is in the other room crying and saying, "Why did she do it?" over and over again. And Ed Gibbs is on the phone trying to get the doctor.

When my mother sees me standing there she motions for the door to be shut.

After the doctor and the ambulance have come and gone, Ed Gibbs puts in a long-distance call to my father. And my older sister walks out the back door and away from the house, across the pasture of tall grass and away from the house, and I follow her, begging her to come back. "Leave me alone!" she says. "Just leave me alone!"

At the funeral parlor my father lifts me up and shows me my mother lying in the casket across the room. I am too heavy for him to hold for long.

If you've got a hook for an arm,
what do you do when you roll up the other sleeve?

        Propped against the wall is a square mirror, flanked by
Cranston Ritchie standing uneasily at attention, both sleeves rolled up to the
elbow; and by a dressmaker's black dummy on a chair, no head, no arms, no legs,
wearing a short slip held on by a safety pin.

Gene's vending machine:
if no answer, call . . .

        If, when you saw the Chicago riots on TV, you wanted
the long-hairs strung up by their balls, you would have to work out something at
home. You could let Christopher go to the rock concert as long as he didn't
contribute to the Panthers. And you could get Jonathan to pose nude in a woman's
mask, a long-haired man emerging from a bathroom with his sex blurred.

Who is he? What is he doing? What does he mean?

For his friend, Mason Randolph, an ex-swimming champion who is afraid to go in the water now.

For his friend, Thomas Merton, who electrocuted himself on a fan in a hotel room in Bangkok.

For his friend, Lester Combs, of Neon, Kentucky, who was struck by lightning and kept the charge in his hand and built an Ark in the creek bed out behind his shack; for Lester Combs, whose wife and children left him building an Ark in a dry creek bed in Neon.

For his friend, Professor Evanston Hughes, whose wife died of cancer and who found dozens of notes from her hidden around the house and who married a student three weeks later.

For his friend, Cranston Ritchie: first they cut off his hand, then they cut off his arm at the elbow, then they cut off his arm at the shoulder; for his friend, Cranston Ritchie, who died young of cancer.

During the summer of 1970 the doctors told Gene Meatyard that he had only a few weeks to live, to prepare to return to the hospital soon to die.

Instead, he went out and bought brightly colored jackets and shirts and ties, and a red, white and blue belt; and for the next two years he tended shop as usual. He lost weight steadily, and toward the end he was so weak that he could not stand for long; but he tended his shop daily without help, and he continued to photograph on the weekends as often as he could.

When he died, the red, white and blue belt—which by then had new holes punched one after another until it wrapped around him nearly twice—was christened "Murcan Courage" by his wife and children and hung on the wall among his photographs in their home in Lexington.

Who is he? What is he doing? What does he mean?

For his wife, Madelyn, who rubs his back at night when he can't sleep. For his son, Michael, and his daughter-in-law, Candy, who at eighteen have a baby and a new car. For his son, Christopher, who is upstairs with the door closed listening to the Beatles. For Melissa, who is too young to be told.

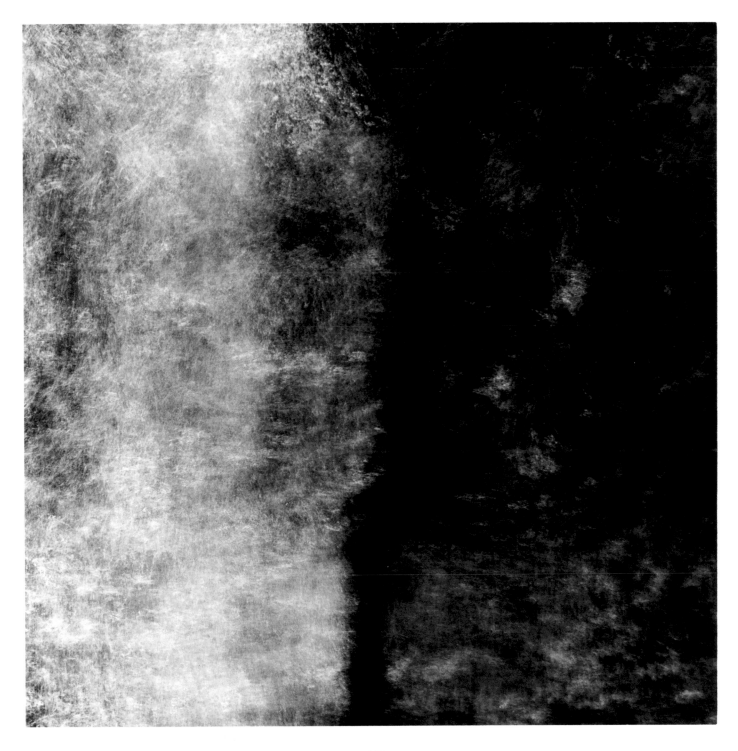

Melissa among the Meatyards.

A child in a great field is crouched in shadow, and the dandelions gone to seed in the darkness catch small lights all around her. And her father, seeing this, puts before her something brighter than dandelions gone to seed: a scarred hubcap from the roadside. It appears then to be a bright table set before her; it appears then to be a bright mirror within her reach, to be a bright world alive beneath her reaching hand. And so they picnic there often during his last years, the whole family, on homemade wine and bread, their reflections bent together in the bright scarred trope between them.

Reminiscence   Guy Davenport

When I moved to Lexington ten years ago the poet Jonathan Williams wrote
me that there was a photographer here who took pictures of children and
American flags in attics. His name was Ralph Eugene Meatyard. He was,
Jonathan insisted, strange. I had learned to trust Jonathan's judgments. When he
said strange he meant strange.

The next time Jonathan was in town, on one of his reading and slide-showing
tours around the Republic in his Volkswagen, The Blue Rider, with its football
decal on a window saying THE POETS (the football team of some Sidney Lanier
High School in the pine fastnesses of Georgia), he and Ronald Johnson, Stan
Brakhage and his six-year-old daughter Crystal, Bonnie Jean Cox and I set out to
visit the Meatyards. The address was 418 Kingsway. We all piled out at 418
Queensway, and to this day I don't know the startled citizens who opened their
door to find such a collection of people on the steps. Jonathan was got up as a
Methodist minister in a three-piece suit, Stan was in his period of looking like a
Pony Express scout out of Frederic Remington, and Bonnie Jean and Crystal were
both gazing innocently up out from under bangs.

We fitted in well enough at the Meatyards' when we got there, a place where
you were liable to find anything at all. There was an original drawing of Andy
Gump crying "Oh, Min!" from the toilet stool: he has no paper. There were
Merzbilden, paintings by the children, found objects, cats and dogs, books
jammed into every conceivable space.

Gene Meatyard was a smiling, affable man of middle age and height. His wife
Madelyn, Scandinavian in her beauty, had a full measure of Midwestern
hospitality to make us feel comfortable. My own welcome was assured when we
heard, as Melissa, the youngest Meatyard, showed her agemate Crystal Brakhage
the kitchen, a little girl's piping voice saying, "Guy Davenport has ants and bugs
in *his* kitchen." This gave me a chance to explain that I kept a saucer of sugar
water for the wasps, hornets and ants that I liked to see in the house. To the
Meatyards it meant that I couldn't be all bad.

Photographs were handed around. We talked about them. But not Gene. For nine years I would see the new pictures as they were printed and mounted, always in complete silence from Gene. He never instructed one how to see, or how to interpret the pictures, or what he might have intended. The room was full of keen eyes: Jonathan's lyric, bawdy eye; Ronald's eye for mystery; Stan's cinematic eye (a bit impatient with still images, as Gene was impatient with Stan's films — he never went to the movies, but would watch television if the program were sufficiently absurd); Bonnie Jean's stubborn, no-nonsense eye.

I did not know until after his death that he brought me the pictures to cheer himself up. "Guy knows what to say," he told Madelyn. I only said what the pictures drew out. I think he liked my having to fall back on analogies: that this print had a touch of Kafka, this a passage as if by Cézanne, this echoed de Chirico. In his last period he was fascinated by Cézanne and the Cubists, by the verbal collages of William Carlos Williams.

We saw a wealth of pictures that evening. I remember thinking that here was a photographer who might illustrate the ghost stories of Henry James, a photographer who got many of his best effects by introducing exactly the right touch of the unusual into an authentically banal American usualness. So much of Gene's work requires the deeper attention which shows you that in a quite handsome picture of lawns and trees there are bricks floating in the air (they have been tied to branches to make them grow level; you cannot see the wires).

Light as it falls from the sun onto our random world defines everything perceptible to the eye by constant accident, relentlessly changing. A splendid spot of light on a fence is gone in a matter of seconds. A tone of light is frailer in essence than a whiff of roses. I have watched Gene all of a day wandering around the ruined Whitehall photographing as diligently as if he were a newsreel cameraman in a battle. The old house was as quiet and still as eternity itself; to Gene it was as ephemeral in its shift of light and shade as a fitful moth.

He developed his film only once a year; he didn't want to be tyrannized by impatience, and I suspect that he didn't like being cooped up in the darkroom. He was a lens grinder by profession, which meant he was short of free time. His evenings were apt to be taken up with teaching, lecturing, arranging shows, and he longed to read more and more. There were books in his automobile, by his equipment in his office. He had more hobbies than could be kept up with, especially those that involved his family: hiking, cooking, collecting the poetic trash that served as props for his pictures. One could usually find the Meatyards up to something rich and strange: making violet jam (or some other sufficiently unlikely flavor), model ships, fanciful book covers; listening to a superb collection of antique jazz, or to recordings which Gene seemed to dream up and then command the existence of, like the Andrews Sisters singing Poe's "Raven" ("Ulalume" on the flip side, both in close harmony). He had a recording of the wedding of Sister Rosetta Tharp. He had a loose-leaf notebook of thousands of grotesque and absurd names. He was a living encyclopedia of bizarre accidents and Kentucky locutions. One evening he turned up to tell with delight of hearing an old man say of the moving pictures these days that by God you can see the actors' genitrotties.

And there was nothing behind him, nothing at all that one could make out. He had invented himself, with his family's full cooperation. One knew that he had been born in Normal, Illinois, because of the comedy of the name. He had a brother, an artist, but it took forever to find this out. He had been to Williams. Williams! Surely this was an invention. Like hearing Harpo Marx had a degree from the Sorbonne. For whereas Gene seemed to read German, he pronounced French like Dr. Johnson—as if it were English. Greek nor Latin had he, though he once figured out with a modern Greek dictionary that a lyric of Sappho (which he had set out to read as his first excursion into the Classics) had something to do with a truck crossing a bridge. Yet, by golly, he had been to Williams College. He was there with the Navy V-12 program. One even learned that he used to play golf. But he had no past. His own past had no interest whatever for him. Tomorrow morning was his great interest.

There was the London Telephone Book to be read (the scholar Tom Stroup sent him one), new books of poetry to read between customers at the eyeglasses shop. He was an unfailing follower-up, which is why I think of him as the best educated man I have ever known. As a professor I must work with people for whom indifference is both a creed and a defense of their fanatic narrowness of mind, but Gene knew nothing of this. When he met Louis and Celia Zukofsky at my house, he went away and read Zukofsky. Not that he was an enthusiast. He simply had a curiosity that went all the way, and a deep sense of courtesy whereby if a man were a writer he would read what he had written, if a man were a painter he would look at his paintings.

Gene's extraordinary difference from any type sometimes puzzled people when they first met him. One evening the Montaigne scholar Marcel Gutwirth was in town, and he and Gene and I had a marvelous evening of talk while watching a new litter of kittens spring around the living room. When I walked Professor Gutwirth back to his hotel afterwards, he asked *who* this Monsieur Meatyard might be.

"Oh, Gene's wonderful," I said. "He knows more about modern literature than anyone at the university, but he's never read the *Odyssey*."

"But, *ah!*" Marcel Gutwirth said. "What a reading the *Odyssey* will have when he gets around to it!"

Gene took up photography in 1954 and began to love it enough to submit to the demands it was making. He must have seen the difference between a photographer and an artist whose medium is photography. After a heart attack in 1961, he gave himself ten years to master his art. He was a great photographer well before that decade was up.

My first experience of Gene at work came when I asked him to do some pictures of me for the covers of a book. I had already selected a rich picture of his that I wanted for the front cover (the book was *Flowers and Leaves*), and we needed a portrait for the back. Gene drove me over to Interstate Highway 75 on a Sunday afternoon and put me out in the middle of traffic. He parked on the shoulder and began to photograph me trying to dodge a Greyhound bus and other dashing objects. I have never seen these pictures. Then he took me to an old churchyard and photographed me among the headstones. Finally, he drove to a house gutted by fire, and here he made the picture which we used. He never explained any of these settings. I only knew that he was after essence, not fact.

Usually he photographed people in so casual a manner that one did not know he was at work. I can remember three wonderful conversations with Thomas Merton, one of Gene's closest friends, which were recorded in this way. Gene never dropped out of the talk to find an angle, never asked anyone to pose. The camera was simply there. And, afterwards, the pictures.

He was rare among American artists in that he was not obsessed with his own image in the world. He could therefore live in perfect privacy in a rotting Kentucky town. He was forever sending off shows, he kept up with everything, he encouraged everybody. He was a quiet, diffident, charming person on the surface, a known ruse of the American genius (William Carlos Williams, Marianne Moore). This modesty amounted to there being at least two distinct Gene Meatyards in the world: an invisible Lexington businessman and a genius who achieved one of the most beautiful styles in twentieth-century art.

His death, heroic and tragic, proved to be the occasion for recognizing the two Gene Meatyards. For two funerals were required. The first was Protestant and, despite the distinguished people who came from all over the United States, thoroughly dull. I felt, as Cocteau had at another such obsequy, that Gene had not cared to attend. It was so formulaic and uninspired that I had to go and stand with my hands flat against the coffin to assure myself that I was at a funeral at all.

But there was another funeral, a true Meatyard funeral, one at which the rites were made up out of the family fund of inventiveness. A small group of us, Madelyn, the children (Mike with his wife and child, Christopher and Melissa), Joy Little, Bob May, Jonathan Greene, Bonnie Jean and I, went into the Red River Gorge which Gene had explored and photographed and tried to save from the ravagements of politics and greed. It was a fine spring Sunday. We climbed to an eminence that Gene had liked, a place as remote and quiet as any forest that had not yet heard the buzz saw and the bulldozer. Here we drank a wine that Gene had brewed. I read aloud a poem that Christopher had written, Mike emptied the canister that held all that could die and be burnt of Gene over the ledge of the high rock—a few dry bones which sifted into the tall treetops below. Melissa cast after them a bagful of flower petals.

Then we walked to another part of the forest and ate a feast, picnic fare of the outrageously copious and toothsome and rich kind which Gene fancied for a proper outing. Had Homer been a Sybarite, he would have described such a meal: chilled wines and cold chicken, crisp vinegary salads and homemade bread. I cannot describe it for I don't think I got to see it all, the choices were so great. I remember that when we could eat no more there were still plums swimming in port passed around in small round glasses.

And this funeral Gene attended.

CHRONOLOGY

1925   Born May 15 in Normal, Illinois.

1943   Graduated from high school and entered Navy V-12 program at Williams College; stayed one year.

1946   Discharged from Navy; married Madelyn McKinney; apprenticed as optician in Chicago.

1949   Became licensed optician; worked for Gailey Eye Clinic in Bloomington, Illinois.

1950   First child born (Michael); quit Gailey Eye Clinic and went back to school on G.I. Bill at Illinois Wesleyan University; left after one semester to take job as optician with Tinder-Krauss-Tinder in Lexington, Kentucky; bought first camera to take pictures of Michael.

1954   Took class in photography under Van Deren Coke; joined Lexington Camera Club and Photographic Society of America; bought secondhand Leica.

1955   Second child born (Christopher); showed in PSA salons; acquired Rolleiflex.

1956   Hung in "Creative Photography" with Adams, White, Siskind, Callahan, the Westons, and others— show organized by Van Deren Coke; attended summer photography workshop in Bloomington, Indiana, studied with Henry Holmes Smith and Minor White.

1957   Two-man show with Van Deren Coke at A Photographer's Gallery in New York City.

1959   First one-man show, Tulane University; third child born (Melissa); portfolio and article about him by Coke published in Aperture.

1961   Selected by Beaumont Newhall for inclusion in "New Talent in Photography USA" section of *Art in America*, Vol. 49, No. 1; suffered heart attack, discovered he had had gout for years; was bedridden for six weeks, inactive for six months.

1967   Opened own optical business in Lexington (Eyeglasses of Kentucky).

1967   Hiked and camped in Red River Gorge with Wendell Berry in their collaboration on *The*
1970   *Unforeseen Wilderness.*

1970   Monograph prepared and published by Jonathan Greene of Gnomon Press; discovered that he had terminal cancer; began Lucybelle Crater pictures with book in mind.

1972   Died May 7 at home in Lexington.

PUBLISHED PHOTOGRAPHS

COLLECTIONS

Ralph Eugene Meatyard. Lexington, Kentucky, Gnomon Press, 1970.

The Family Album of Lucybelle Crater. Jargon Press, 1974. Text by Jonathan Williams and others.

The Unforeseen Wilderness. Lexington, Kentucky, University of Kentucky Press, 1971. Text by Wendell Berry.

BOOK AND PERIODICAL SELECTIONS

Amanuensis, Vol. 2, No. 2 (Fall 1973).

American Association for the Advancement of Science Bulletin, Vol. 14, No. 2.

Art of Photography, The, Time-Life series.

Artforum, Vol. IV, No. 5 (January 1966).

Artweek, Vol. 3, No. 40.

Audubon (May 1971).

Be-ing Without Clothes (1970).

Big Rock Candy Mountain, Vol. 2, No. 1.

blue-tail fly, Vol. 1, Nos. 2, 6, and 8.

Courier Journal and Times Magazine (December 8,

1957; February 1, 1959; April 18 and July 4, 1971).

Encyclopedia of Photography, The, Vol. 19.

Floating Opera, The, Vol. 3, No. 2.

Hudson Review, Vol. XXIII, No. 4.

Image, Vol. 15, No. 2.

Kentucky 69, into 70, University of Kentucky Yearbook.

Kentucky Kernel, The (October 26, 1970).

Light[7] (1968).

Man in the Poetic Mode, Joy Zweigler, ed.

Maps—Zukofsky, John Taggart, ed.

Motive (October 1967).

Our University, University of Kentucky (November 1966).

Photographing Children, Time-Life series.

Photography/1973, Time-Life series.

Photo Reporter, The, Vol. 3, Issue 3 (March 1973).

Photo World, Vol. 2, No. 3 (March 1974).

San Francisco Chronicle (November 21, 1972).

TriQuarterly, No. 19 (Fall 1970). Reprinted in book form by David Lewis, *Edward Dahlberg. A Tribute.*

Whole Earth Catalog (March 1970).

DUST JACKET PORTRAITS

Wendell Berry, for *A Continuous Harmony* and *The Country of Marriage.*

Guy Davenport, for *Flowers and Leaves.*

Thomas Merton, for *Thomas Merton—Social Critic.*

Jonathan Williams, for *Jonathan Williams, Poet.*

Louis Zukofsky, for *Maps—Zukofsky* and *Autobiography.*

BOOK COVERS

Flowers and Leaves, Guy Davenport.

Older Rural Americans, E. Grant Youmans, ed.

Openings, Wendell Berry.

Spring of the Lamb, Douglas Woolf.

ANNOUNCEMENTS AND CATALOGUES

Carl Siembab Gallery show, REM, 1962.

Columbia College show, REM, 1971.

"Contemporary Photographer," 1961.

"Creative Photography," 1956.

Matrix show, REM, 1972.

"Multiple Image," Rhode Island School of Design, 1972.

Photographer's Gallery show, REM and Van Deren Coke, 1957.

"Photography, 1968."

"Photography, 1970."

"Photography '72."

Picker Gallery show, REM, 1971.

Quivira Gallery show, REM and Van Deren Coke, 1968.

Steinrock Gallery show, REM, 1971.

"Thirty Photographers," 1964.

Witkin Gallery show, REM, 1973.

PRINTS IN PUBLIC COLLECTIONS

George Eastman House, Rochester, New York

Massachusetts Institute of Technology, Cambridge, Massachusetts

Metropolitan Museum of Art, New York, New York

Museum of Modern Art, New York, New York

Pasadena Art Museum, Pasadena, California

Smithsonian Institution, Washington, D.C.

Thomas Merton Studies Center, Louisville, Kentucky

University of California at Los Angeles, California

University of Louisville, Louisville, Kentucky

University of Nebraska, Lincoln, Nebraska

University of New Mexico, Albuquerque, New Mexico

Visual Studies Workshop, Rochester, New York

ONE-MAN SHOWS

1959   Tulane University, New Orleans, Louisiana

1961   Morehead State College, Morehead, Kentucky
University of Florida, Gainesville, Florida

1962   Carl Siembab Gallery, Boston, Massachusetts
University of Florida, Gainesville, Florida

1963   Arizona State University, Tempe, Arizona
University of Florida, Gainesville, Florida

1965   University of New Mexico, Albuquerque, New Mexico

1966   Arizona State University, Tempe, Arizona

1967   Bellarmine College, Louisville, Kentucky
University of New Mexico, Albuquerque, New Mexico

1968   Doctor's Park, Lexington, Kentucky

1970   Center for Photographic Studies, Louisville, Kentucky
Ohio University, Athens, Ohio
Student Center Gallery, University of Kentucky, Lexington, Kentucky

1971   Chicago Art Institute, Chicago, Illinois
George Eastman House, Rochester, New York
J. B. Speed Museum, Louisville, Kentucky
Jefferson Community College, Watertown, New York
Massachusetts Institute of Technology, Cambridge, Massachusetts
Picker Gallery, Colgate University, Hamilton, New York
Steinrock Gallery, Lexington, Kentucky

1972   Charles W. Bowers Memorial Museum, Santa Ana, California
Columbia College, Chicago, Illinois
Cortland Free Library, Cortland, New York
Doctor's Park, Lexington, Kentucky
Focus Gallery, San Francisco, California
Light Impressions, Rochester, New York
Logan Helm Woodford County Library, Versailles, Kentucky
Matrix, Hartford, Connecticut
Northeast Louisiana State College, Monroe, Louisiana
Watson Gallery, Elmira College, Elmira, New York

1973   Cincinnati Art Academy, Cincinnati, Ohio
University of Delaware, Newark, Delaware
Witkin Gallery, New York, New York

1974   Colorado Springs Fine Arts Center, Colorado Springs, Colorado
Oakton College, Morton Grove, Illinois

TWO-MAN SHOWS

1957   *(with Van Deren Coke)* A Photographer's Gallery, New York, New York

1967   *(with Walt Lowe)* J. B. Speed Museum, Louisville, Kentucky

1968   *(with Van Deren Coke)* Quivira Gallery, Corrales, New Mexico

1974   *(with Henry Holmes Smith)* J. B. Speed Museum, Louisville, Kentucky

GROUP SHOWS

1954 "Second Southeastern Salon of Photography,"
1954 International Exhibition, Orlando, Florida
"Seventh Hartford International Exhibition of
Photography," Wadsworth Atheneum, Hartford,
Connecticut

1955 "Bergen County International Exhibition of
Photography," Bergen County, New Jersey
"Light and Shadow International," Rosicrucian
Art Gallery, San Jose, California
"Northwest International Photographic Salon,"
Puyllup, Washington
"Seattle International Exhibition of Photog-
raphy," Seattle Art Museum, Seattle, Wash-
ington

1956 "Creative Photography," University of Kentucky, Lexington, Kentucky

1958 "Coke Collection," Indiana University, Bloomington, Indiana

1959 "Photographer's Choice," Indiana University,
Bloomington, Indiana
"Sense of Abstraction," Museum of Modern Art,
New York, New York

1960 "Fotografie della Nuova Generazione," Milan,
Italy

1961 Arizona State University, Tempe, Arizona
"Photo Show," Arts in Louisville Gallery,
Louisville, Kentucky
"Six Photographers," University of Illinois,
Urbana, Illinois

1962 "Photography U.S.," de Cordova Museum, Lincoln, Massachusetts
"Rhode Island Arts Festival"

1963 "Photography 63/An International Exhibition,"
George Eastman House, Rochester, New York

1964 "30 Photographers," State University of New
York at Buffalo, New York

1966 "American Photography: The Sixties," Sheldon
Memorial Art Gallery, University of Nebraska,
Lincoln, Nebraska

1967 "Photography International," San Jose State
College, San Jose, California
"Photography in the Twentieth Century,"
traveling exhibition by George Eastman House
for National Gallery of Canada

1968 "Contemporary Photographs," University of
California at Los Angeles, California
"Five Photographers," University of Nebraska,
Lincoln, Nebraska
"Photography 1968," Morlan Gallery, Transyl-
vania College, Lexington, Kentucky

1969 "Light⁷," Massachusetts Institute of Technology,
Cambridge, Massachusetts
"Photographs from the Coke Collection,"
Albuquerque Art Museum, Albuquerque, New
Mexico
"Recent Acquisitions," Pasadena Art Museum,
Pasadena, California

1969 "The Camera and the Human Façade," Smith-
–70 sonian Institution, Washington, D.C.

1970 "Photographs for Sale," Visual Studies Workshop,
Rochester, New York
"Photography, 1970," Morlan Gallery, Transyl-
vania College, Lexington, Kentucky

1971 "Photographs from the Coke Collection,"
Everson Museum of Art, Syracuse, New York

1972 Florissant College, St. Louis, Missouri
"Photography '72," J. B. Speed Museum, Louis-
ville, Kentucky
"The Multiple Image," Creative Photography
Gallery, Massachusetts Institute of Technology,
Cambridge, Massachusetts
"The Multiple Image," Rhode Island School of
Design, Providence, Rhode Island

1973 "1972–73 New Acquisitions," University of New
Mexico, Albuquerque, New Mexico

PUBLISHED WRITINGS: BY RALPH EUGENE MEATYARD

"Remembering F. v.d. C." *The Kentucky Review,* Vol. 2 (Autumn 1969), pp. 49–51.

"Statement." *Photographer's Choice,* No. 1 (Spring 1959). Pamphlet accompanying show by same name,
Bloomington, Indiana.

"Thomas Merton Eulogized: 'Very Much with World.'" *The Kentucky Kernel,* Vol. LX, No. 72 (December 13, 1968), p. 2.

PUBLISHED WRITINGS
ABOUT RALPH EUGENE MEATYARD

Albright, Thomas, Review of show at Focus Gallery, 1972. San Francisco *Chronicle* (November 21, 1972), p. 43.

Berry, Wendell, "Note," in *Ralph Eugene Meatyard* (Lexington, Kentucky, Gnomon Press, 1970).

Block, Lou, "Meatyard Manifesto — The Coughing PSA." *Gazette of the Arts in Louisville,* I:18, pp. 1–2.

Coke, Van Deren, "The Photographs of Eugene Meatyard." *Aperture,* VII:4 (Winter), pp. 154–68.

Coleman, A. D., "From Dolls and Masks to Lynchings." Review of show at Witkin Gallery, 1973. *New York
Times* (March 11, 1973).

————, "Latent Image." *Village Voice* (February 18, 1971), p. 16.

Davenport, Guy, "Ralph Eugene Meatyard: Eight Photographs." *The Kentucky Review*, Vol. II, No. 1 (February 1968).

Deschin, Jacob. Review of show at Photographer's Gallery, 1957. *New York Times* (January 6, 1957), V18.

————. Review of show at Witkin Gallery, 1973. *The Photo Reporter,* Vol. 3, Issue 3 (March 1973), p. 11.

Gassan, Arnold, "Note," in *Ralph Eugene Meatyard* (Lexington, Kentucky, Gnomon Press, 1970).

Hall, James Baker. Review of *The Unforeseen Wilderness, Big Rock Candy Mountain*, Vol. 2, No. 1.

————, "The Strange New World of Ralph Eugene Meatyard." *Popular Photography*, LXV:1 (July 1969), pp. 120, 146.

Kielkopf, Larry, "Meatyard's Photos Are Hauntingly Personal." Review of *Ralph Eugene Meatyard* (Gnomon Press Monograph). *The Kentucky Kernel* (October 23, 1970), p. 3.

Lansdell, Sara, "Meatyard, Gaines, and Langdon Surface on Tide of Art Activity." Louisville *Courier Journal and Times* (October 18, 1970), F16.

————, "Seeing Wilderness on Its Own Terms." Review of Red River Gorge show, J. B. Speed Museum. Louisville *Courier Journal and Times* (June 1971).

Murray, Joan. Review of show at Focus Gallery, 1972. *Artweek,* Vol. 3, No. 40 (November 25, 1972), p. 9.

Rannels, Edward W., "Photography 1968 at Transylvania." Lexington *Herald-Leader* (March 10, 1968).

Wright, George, "A Vote of Confidence for Coke and Meatyard." *Village Voice* (January 30, 1957).

MISCELLANEOUS MATERIALS

Portfolio One. Center for Photographic Studies, Louisville, Kentucky, 1972. Portfolio dedicated to REM; contains one REM photograph printed by Alex Traube, signed by REM.

Portfolio Three/Ralph Eugene Meatyard. Center for Photographic Studies. Ten prints made by C. J. Pressma; introduction by Van Deren Coke. One hundred copies, numbered, unsigned.

Tape of talk and discussion accompanying slide show of Lucybelle Crater pictures. Midwest Society for Photographic Education Conference, University of Louisville, 1972. Tape and slides in possession of University of Louisville.

Slides of Visual Studies Workshop Traveling Ralph Eugene Meatyard show. For sale through "The Walrus," Box 782, Rochester, New York 14603; $40 per set, unmounted.

PHOTOGRAPH BY JAMES BAKER HALL
Made with a Nikon Camera
Nikon, Inc., Garden City, New York
Subsidiary of Ehrenreich Photo-Optical Industries, Inc.

PHOTOGRAPH BY DAVID AKIBA
Made with a Hasselblad Camera
Exclusive United States Distributor of Hasselblad
SLR Cameras and Accessories:
Paillard, Incorporated,
1900 Lower Road
Linden, New Jersey 07036

SUSTAINING SUBSCRIBERS

A. M. Bullowa, New York, New York
Shirley C. Burden, Beverly Hills, California
Kate Dayton, Minneapolis, Minnesota
Geoffrey Gund, New Haven, Connecticut
Edward Powis Jones, New York, New York
Tim Loomis, Middleburg, Virginia
David McAlpin, Princeton, New Jersey
Jim McCrary, Panorama City, California
Barbara M. Marshall, Chestnut Hill, Massachusetts
Mr. & Mrs. Beaumont Newhall, Albuquerque, New Mexico
The Norman Foundation, New York, New York
Gerald H. Robinson, Portland, Oregon
Paul & Hazel Strand, Yvelines, France
Robert Allan Taub, Dearborn, Michigan

RETAINING SUBSCRIBERS

Maria Glaser Ackley, Mercer Island, Washington
Ansel Adams, Carmel, California
Jack & Susan Ahearn, Red Hook, New York
Neale M. Albert, New York, New York
Dan Alexander, Bakersfield, California
Devereaux Barnes, Wilmington, Delaware
James P. Baxter, Chicago, Illinois
Arthur Bell, Chicago, Illinois
Llewellyn L. Berry III, Washington, D. C.
Mr. & Mrs. David A. Blanchard, Fort Lauderdale, Florida
Ms. Gete Bond, Boulder, Colorado
Scott F. Brown, Exeter, New Hampshire
Taber Chadwick, Chicago, Illinois
Wayne Coombs, Morgantown, West Virginia
Julian Cottrell, London, England
Tippy D'Auria, Miami, Florida
James F. Davis, Woodstock, New York
Robert Overton Day, New York, New York
John Delacour, Pyrmont NSW, Australia
Harry Casimir de Rahm, Cambridge, Massachusetts
Allen T. Dittman, Garrett Park, Maryland
Helen Doroshow, Sante Fe, New Mexico
Joan Pyle Dufault, New York, New York
Mac & Eugenie Dupont, Beverly, Massachusetts
Charles T. Easley, Waco, Texas
Elaine Ellman, New York, New York
Gary Farah, Belleville, New Jersey
Charles & Elissa Forbes, West Hawley, Massachusetts
Albert R. Frederick, Jr., M.D., Wellesley Hills, Massachusetts
George B. Fry III, Atherton, California
Mr. & Mrs. Robert Gage, Pound Ridge, New York

James Garland, Bowie, Maryland
Martin Gavler, Osterskar, Sweden
Arnold M. Gilbert, Flossmoor, Illinois
Anthony Graham, Montreal, Canada
Martus Granirer, New York, New York
C. Guildner, M.D., Snohomish, Washington
Katharine Gust, Sausalito, California
Peter E. Haas, Jr., Novato, California
Wilfrid Hamlin, Plainfield, Vermont
Ray W. Hawksley, Richmond, California
Ralph M. Hower, Weston, Massachusetts
Kenneth Stephen Hulbert, La Mesa, California
Louise Irvin, Oakland, California
Richard Kehrwald, Sheridan, Wyoming
The Rev. T. K. Kunichika, Hawaii Preparatory Academy, Kamuela, Hawaii
Gordon Lee, M.D., Glenwood, Minnesota
Russell Lee, Austin, Texas
Ben Maddow, Los Angeles, California
Gerald R. Martin, Minneapolis, Minnesota
Philip Masnick, New York, New York
Charles Matlin, Sacramento, California
Neil E. Matthew, Indianapolis, Indiana
Jack & Annemarie Maynard, Newport, Michigan
Ralph Eugene Meatyard, Lexington, Kentucky
Daniel McCormack, Accord, New York
Richard L. Menschel, New York, New York
Robert Menschel, New York, New York
Frank Minutillo, Bolton, Connecticut
Sheila Mahoney Morgenstern, Rochester, New York
Stephen E. Myers, Akron, Ohio
Sherwood Omens, North Hollywood, California
Robert C. Page, M.D., Richardson, Texas
John M. Perko, St. Louis, Missouri
Bernard Quint, New York, New York
Jeffry Reynolds, Tampa, Florida
David C. Ruttenberg, Chicago, Illinois
Joseph and Pamela Saltzer, Mount Kisco, New York
Stephen Shore, New York, New York
Robert William Slack, Dayton, Ohio
Spencer L. Snyder, Los Angeles, California
Anthony E. Spare, Hillsborough, California
William P. Steele, New York, New York
George Stranahan, M.D., Woody Creek, Colorado
Aaron Sussman, New York, New York
Carol Tierney, Toronto, Canada
Jim Tonery, Rochester, New York
Joseph L. Tucker, Clayton, Missouri
James G. Waters, Arlington, Virginia
Ernst L. Wehausen, Denver, Colorado
Stephen Williams, Filmcom, Berwyn, Pennsylvania
James A. Wilson, M.D., Athens, Ohio
Edith and Robert Worth, Nutley, New Jersey